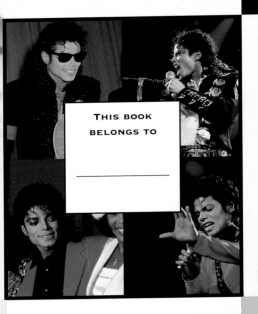

THIS BOOK
BELONGS TO

_____

MICHAEL

BY

THERESA CELSI

• ARIEL BOOKS •

ANDREWS AND

McMEEL

KANSAS CITY

JACKSON

Cover photo: Vinnie Zuffante / Star File

All photographs courtesy of the Star File Photo Agency and their photographers: Max Goldstein, Todd Kaplan, Vinnie Zuffante, Tony Gale, Dagmar, Chuck Pulia, Gene Shaw, Danny Chin.

ISBN: 0-8362-3044-2

Library of Congress Catalog Card Number: 93-70469

MICHAEL
JACKSON

"CERTAIN PEOPLE WERE CREATED FOR CERTAIN THINGS, AND I THINK OUR JOB IS TO ENTERTAIN THE WORLD."

On May 16, 1983, Americans tuned their televisions to the musical event of the year: Motown, the legendary record company that had revolutionized popular music in the 1960s and 1970s, was celebrating its twenty-fifth

anniversary. Berry Gordy, Jr., founder of the company, had made stars out of Diana Ross, Marvin Gaye, Gladys Knight, and the Jackson Five.

The Jackson Five sang together in public for the first time since all of them, except Jermaine, had left Motown. But the one Jackson everyone tuned in to see was Michael. The Jackson brothers, Jackie, Tito, Jermaine, Marlon, Michael, and Randy, sang a medley of their hits from the Motown years. Then Michael was left alone onstage.

"Those were the good songs," Michael said in his soft voice. "I like those songs a lot. But especially, I like the *new* songs." The stage went dark, and the opening riff from his No. 1 hit "Billie Jean" started. The crowd went wild as Michael began to sing and dance. He did his signature Moonwalk, gliding backwards, spinning around three times like a figure skater, and stopping on his toes. He was aflame on the floor! At the end of the song, the audience gave the performer a standing ovation.

MICHAEL JACKSON

Michael's performance was the culmination of nearly twenty years of experience that began when he was a child. And it was also a beginning. It symbolized a coming of age. Michael was alone in his stardom now. The Jacksons were all princes, but in that brief, shining moment, Michael left them behind and ascended the throne as the King of Pop.

A GROUP FROM GARY

Born in 1958, Michael Jackson was one of nine children growing up in a small two-

bedroom house in Gary, Indiana. His greatest passion was playing practical jokes, and his main talent was avoiding punishment when caught.

His parents, Joseph and Katherine, were both musicians. Joseph played guitar in a band for extra income, but mostly for the pleasure. His one precious possession was his guitar, which he forbade his children to touch. Sometimes, though, when he was gone, Katherine would play for the children and sing with them.

One day, the television broke. With

A GROUP
FROM GARY

no entertainment handy, the boys couldn't resist taking Joseph's guitar out. In time, seven-year-old Tito managed to learn a few chords. The boys were very careful with the guitar, but inevitably one of the strings snapped. Now Joseph was sure to find out they had touched his beloved instrument.

At first, Joseph was angry. Then Tito played for him while the others sang. Joseph suddenly had a vision of his sons singing together on a stage. The next day, he came home with a new red electric guitar for Tito.

From that day on, promoting the boys became the focus of the family. Joseph spent every penny he could on musical instruments. He taught the boys everything he knew. At first, the group was made up of Jackie, Tito, and Jermaine. Marlon joined a couple of years later. One day in

1963, Katherine heard five-year-old Michael singing and was amazed at how strong and beautiful his voice was. She suggested that Michael not only join the group but also sing lead.

The group, called Ripples and Waves Plus Michael, started competing in talent shows. They won contest after contest as far away as Chicago. Before long, the house was filled with trophies.

"MICHAEL HAS A LOT OF PEOPLE A

KNOW WHY. I THINK IT COMES FROM T

HIM, BUT HE'S VERY AFRAID. I DON'T

Y DAYS." — DIANA ROSS

By 1964, the group, now called the Jackson Five, was playing professional gigs. It was a strange experience for the children—some of the places they played were burlesque houses and strip joints.

While the older boys couldn't wait to finish the shows and get back to their rooms, Michael watched the other entertainers to see what they did onstage. His brothers saw the gigs simply as work; Michael was learning from them—learning how to dance, how to hold a mike, how to control an audience with his voice.

In 1968, the Jackson Five played the Apollo Theater in New York City. Located in Harlem, the Apollo was the most famous black theater in the country. If you were a hit there, you knew you were among the

best. If you were not, you found that out quickly. The audience was known to throw rotten fruit and vegetables at acts that didn't come up to its standards. The

Jackson Five had nothing to worry about: They received a roaring standing ovation.

Perhaps the legendary magic Michael creates onstage came from a legend at the Apollo. Inside the theater was the trunk of a tree that had once stood outside a Harlem nightclub. Like the Blarney Stone in Ireland, it was said to bestow luck on anyone who touched it. Tradition required that new acts touch the tree just before performing for the first time. One by one as they went onstage, the Jacksons touched the tree, but little Michael ran

back and touched it once more. That second touch may have given him some extra magic that he carries to this day.

MOTOWN

The same year that they played the Apollo, the Jackson Five got an audition at Motown Records. This was the chance they had been working for. Although the boys were to make their first TV appearance, Joseph canceled the booking and loaded the kids in the van, bound for Motown.

As soon as owner Berry Gordy, Jr., saw their audition film, he signed them. Gordy even had an ingenious idea for promoting them. Diana Ross, his top female recording artist, would "discover" the boys, generating publicity for herself as well as for the Jacksons. The boys were flown to Los Angeles to meet Diana Ross at her house, where she held a press party. Michael was awestruck by the glamorous singer.

For the next five years, the boys' time was taken up with recording and touring.

As part of the Motown "family," they were given songs written by the talented Motown songwriters, as well as taught how to dress and act and, most importantly, handle the press. After releasing their first album, *Diana Ross Presents the Jackson 5,* they appeared as guests on TV shows, in a Saturday morning cartoon show, and finally in their own variety show. They also performed weekly in Las Vegas.

For a while, the family tried to keep the boys' lives as normal as possible. Michael and Marlon attended a neighbor-

hood school in Los Angeles, where they were now living. But after a few weeks, they had to stop. The students' reactions to the boys disrupted the classroom, so they had to have a private tutor.

It was a strange life for young Michael. He had never really known anything but singing and performing since he was five. Having a professional career meant practicing for hours every day. There wasn't much time left for him to make friends or even play with toys. But he didn't seem to miss those things. He

was always totally focused on his work.

Sometimes working with his brothers was frustrating for Michael. Although he was the youngest member of the Jackson Five, he had almost as much experience as anyone else. And he had a lot more ideas, yet none of his brothers paid any attention to them. He was the main lead singer and had his own solo albums, but to them he was still just their kid brother.

What was worse, though, was that his family seemed to be breaking up. His oldest sister, Rebbie, had married and moved

THING ABOUT MIKE IS THAT HE LETS THINGS GET TO HIM. HE'S REAL SERIOUS AND SENSITIVE THAT WAY."

—JERMAINE JACKSON

to another state, and his brothers were leaving, too. Tito was the first to marry, in 1972. Soon Jermaine, Jackie, and Marlon followed. By 1975, Michael, Randy, and sisters Janet and LaToya were the only children at home.

The family was beginning to break up professionally as well. Although Motown had made the Jackson Five stars, the company's strict policies were stifling the brothers, especially Michael. The main problem was that Motown refused to let the Jacksons write their own material. The

group felt that they couldn't grow as artists and their career was coming to a standstill.

Joseph decided to take the Jackson Five to another company. He negotiated with Epic Records a deal that allowed the Jacksons to choose their own material, including songs they had written.

Unfortunately, this move forced a break-up within the family. Jermaine had married Hazel Gordy, daughter of Motown owner Berry Gordy, Jr. Jermaine was not only part of Motown's recording "family" but also part of Gordy's real family. He

chose to stay with Motown. The group's name also stayed with Motown, which owned the rights. From that time on, the group was known as the Jacksons.

It was a painful break-up, but pain is sometimes a necessary part of growing. It was time for Michael to assert his independence and fulfill the promise of his early talent. It was time for the child to grow into the man—time for the prince to become a king.

Michael's first step down the road to adulthood was unusual: It was a step into unexplored territory—acting. And, ironically, it was sort of a step backward, since he worked again with Motown.

Motown had purchased the rights to the hit Broadway musical *The Wiz* as a vehicle for Diana Ross, and filming began in 1977. Michael had seen the show several times and loved it. He auditioned for the part of the Scarecrow.

"IT'S A NICE PLACE MICHAEL COMES FROM. I WISH WE COULD ALL SPEND TIME IN THAT WORLD."

— STEVEN SPIELBERG

His family was amazed. Michael was so shy. Why would he want to act in a movie? Why would he want to spend so much time filming in New York, away from his family?

But Michael enjoyed the experience. He loved the fantasy of the picture. He loved the heavy make-up required for his role and began wearing it to avoid fans when he returned to Los Angeles. Most of all he loved working with his idol, Diana Ross.

His main problem with his first acting

"WE CALL MICHAEL JACKSON 'SMELLY'

BECAUSE HE'S SO POLITE AND PROPER

WE CAN'T EVEN GET HIM TO SAY THE

WORD *FUNKY*." — QUINCY JONES

role was his dancing—it was too good. Although he'd never taken dance classes, he could pick up the choreography instantly. Finally, Ross took him aside and asked him not to learn the dances quite so quickly. It seemed he was making the rest of the cast look bad.

In other areas, Michael had a lot to learn. In the film, he read a quotation by Socrates, the ancient Greek philosopher. He first pronounced the name "So-crates" instead of "Sock-ruh-tease." After a moment of silence, Michael heard someone whisper the correct pronunciation. It

was the film's musical director, Quincy Jones. Although he didn't know it, Michael had just met one of the most important people in his life, one who would help him achieve his greatest success.

After *The Wiz*, Michael was bursting with ideas for a new album—one that expressed the ideas his brothers had always ignored. He wanted Quincy Jones to produce it, but he was too shy to ask him directly. So he asked Jones to recommend a producer and when Jones suggested himself, Michael hired him eagerly.

The resulting album, *Off the Wall*, sold 10 million copies and boasted four hits. "Don't Stop 'Til You Get Enough"

won Michael a Best Male R&B Vocal Grammy in 1980.

Michael's next album, *Thriller*, was more than an album, it was a phenomenon. Released in 1982, it sold more than 40 million copies, far more than any other album in history. It was the No. 1 album in the United States for thirty-seven weeks in a row, produced seven Top Ten singles, and received twelve Grammy nominations—a record number. That year, Michael took home eight Grammys, more than any other performer in the awards' history.

One song from *Thriller*, "Billie Jean," was important to all African-American artists. The video's success convinced MTV, the music cable station, to show videos by other black artists. Before MTV aired "Billie Jean," its executives didn't feel that music by a black artist could be popular enough to justify air time.

Almost immediately after "Billie Jean," "Beat It" reached number one on the charts. Michael's video of this song cost nearly $200,000 (at a time when most videos cost under $20,000) and used real-

life gang members with dancers to communicate an antiviolence message. The song was so popular that the U.S. government used it as part of its campaign against drunk driving. Michael received a humanitarian award from then President and Mrs. Reagan for the song's use.

Michael asked John Landis, director of *An American Werewolf in London*, to direct the video of "Thriller," in which Michael changed into a werewolf and danced with an assortment of ghosts and ghouls. The video became very expensive.

To help cover costs, Michael made a documentary, *The Making of Michael Jackon's Thriller*, and released it as a home video.

The Jehovah's Witnesses church officials were disturbed by the satanic implications of the video and pressured Michael to reject the song. Both Michael and his mother are devout members of the church. Michael had even done missionary work for it. Threatened with expulsion from the church, Michael added a disclaimer to the video and stopped performing the song.

But no matter. By the time Michael stepped onstage at Motown's twenty-fifth anniversary, he had already made the most successful album of all time. He had more

THE HITS
KEEP COMIN'

"MICHAEL, MAY I HAVE

A BANANA, PLEASE?"

— BUBBLES

deals for albums and endorsements in the works. He was known worldwide. He should have been on top of the world. But was he?

RUMORS FLY

As an artist, Michael Jackson had reached a certain maturity. As a person, he seemed childlike, as if he were making up for the childhood he had missed. At that time he still lived with his parents and filled the house with a whole zoo of exotic pets, including a pet monkey named Bubbles. He

loved going to Disneyland, sneaking through the back doors to avoid being mobbed by fans. He seemed to prefer spending time with children rather than with adults. Among his favorite friends were child-actor Emmanuel Lewis and Ryan White, a child who had contracted AIDS.

To the outside world, his habits seemed strange. Rumors started: That he was gay. That he'd had nose jobs to look like Diana Ross. That he was having a sex-change operation in order to marry actor Clifton Davis. That he slept in an oxygen

tank to stay young. That he and his sister Janet were the same person.

At first, Michael shrugged off these stories. They made him more mysterious, and he liked to keep people guessing. However, as the rumors grew, he became upset. Children, his favorite fans, were too young to realize how absurd these tales were.

To squash the rumors, he issued a press statement asserting his heterosexuality and denying some of the stranger claims about his plastic surgery. Unfortunately, these rumors still persist.

The unbelievable rumors following him had little effect on Michael's popularity. They certainly didn't stop Pepsi-Cola from signing a record-breaking endorsement deal with him for $5 million. The deal was for two commercials using "Billie Jean," with special lyrics written for Pepsi. Michael felt uncomfortable making the commercials because he did not drink Pepsi, so he insisted that he not be shown holding or drinking the product.

During the filming, Michael was to walk down a set of stairs, with flares exploding behind him. Unfortunately, one of the explosions set his hair on fire. His bodyguard quickly put out the fire, but Michael received second- and third-degree burns on the back of his head. By the time

an ambulance arrived to take him to the hospital, rumors were flying that Michael had been assassinated. Michael, wearing his trademark glove, waved to the crowds to reassure them he was all right.

Before he left the hospital, Michael visited the other burn patients. He donated to the hospital the $1.5 million Pepsi paid him because of the accident. Hospital officials gratefully named a wing the Michael Jackson Burn Center.

Besides paying Jackson's fee, Pepsi also agreed to sponsor a music tour that

A COMMERCIAL
DISASTER

would bring the brothers together again.
Michael's appearance in the Victory Tour
was more for his brothers' sakes than for
his own. He was eager to get on to new
projects.

A WORLDWIDE SUCCESS

Michael's next project was one of the most
important events of the 1980s. Ethiopia
was suffering from a terrible famine. Bob
Geldof, of the Boomtown Rats, had galva-
nized the U.K. rock community to raise
money by recording a song whose proceeds

would go toward helping the famine victims.

In the United States, Michael Jackson and Lionel Ritchie wrote "We Are the World," Quincy Jones arranged the music, and a group of international rock superstars cut the single. The song was played simultaneously on radio stations across the country during the Hands Across America event and was also included on an album with other songs donated by recording artists. The project raised nearly $40 million for the famine relief.

A WORLDWIDE SUCCESS

"MICHAEL [IS] AN EXTREMELY FRAG

IN LIFE, MAKING CONTACT WITH PE

HAVING TO BE WORRIED WHITHER GOE

SON. I THINK THAT JUST GETTING ON

S HARD ENOUGH TO HIM, MUCH LESS

WORLD." — JANE FONDA

Working again with Quincy Jones, Michael tried to exceed the success of *Thriller* with a new album, *Bad*. But *Bad* sold "only" 17 million copies. Most people would be ecstatic over sales like that, but Michael had dreamed of selling 100 million. He spent a vast sum of money on its promotional video, most of which went toward *Moonwalker*, a compilation home video.

Even though the videos didn't make back the money he had spent on them,

Michael was on a financial roll. He purchased ATV Music, the company that owned the rights to many of the Beatles' songs, and signed a $28-million deal with Nike to endorse a line of shoes. After a successful *Bad* tour, he renegotiated his contract with CBS (now owned by Sony) and received an advance of $18 million for his next album, plus his own company, Nation Records.

And more fame followed fortune. Michael was named Artist of the Decade by the American Cinema Award Foun-

dation and the Soul Train Music Awards. He also received the first Michael Jackson Award from BMI.

Without stopping to breathe, Michael recorded the *Dangerous* album, filmed its three accompanying videos, and launched its world tour.

The most interesting of the *Dangerous* videos was "Black and White" because of the computer animation technique, "morphing," it used. This magical effect was used to blend the faces of people of different ethnicities into one another, making it

impossible to see where one face ended and the other began. Visually, it made the point about which Michael was singing: Black or white, we are all the same.

"In the Closet," another video from *Dangerous*, marked Michael's co-directorial debut. Filmed in the desert in sepia tones, it showed Michael dancing with supermodel Naomi Campbell. But many fans found the video disappointing because it was not as spectacular as his others.

The 1993 Super Bowl had millions of fans tuned in—and not all were football fans. Michael Jackson's halftime show was a spectacular display of posing, dancing, singing, and fireworks. Hundreds of children sang with him onstage.

In February of that year, Michael made an even bigger appearance—giving his first interview in more than ten years to Oprah Winfrey on national TV. Oprah interviewed Michael on his ranch, where

he walked her through the amusement park he had built for the unfortunate children he regularly brings to his estate for a day of fun. Then he showed her his theater, where beds have been installed so that children who are too ill to sit up can enjoy a show.

During the interview, Michael tried to shed light on such matters as his nose jobs, his changing skin color, and his dating Brooke Shields. When asked about controversial family situations LaToya had written about, Michael demurely replied

that he hadn't read her book and couldn't comment on it. Elizabeth Taylor showed up to talk about the hardships of their similar child-performer backgrounds.

For days after the interview, there were discussions throughout the media about whether Michael had been truthful. But despite the personal mystery of Michael Jackson, there is no question about his public acts of art and charity.

Michael is especially concerned about children all over the world, so he has formed a charity organization, Heal

the World. He raised $20 million for his charity in 1992 by selling HBO the rights to broadcast a concert from his worldwide Dangerous Tour, which made stops in Africa, Japan, Germany, and Romania.

While in Africa, Michael was crowned King of Sani by the village of Krindjavbo, on the Ivory Coast of West Africa. In many ways, he embodies the best qualities of a king. He is not a political leader, yet he inspires others in a positive way. Although many people find him strange, he is a good role model for young

people, refusing to drink or take drugs and opposing sex before marriage. He is also benevolent with his time and wealth. He visits sick children and brings them to visit him. And he is a leader in his work, particularly his videos, which continue to break new artistic ground.

If a king is a person who inspires his subjects, who stands above the crowd and shows what can be accomplished, then Michael Jackson is worthy of that name.

■ When he has his hair trimmed, Michael has the cuttings collected in bags to keep the barber from selling his hair to fans.

■ After the Victory Tour, Michael was offered $10 million to perform in Korea with his brothers. A $1-million bonus was offered to the family member who could convince him to perform.

■ "Muscles," a song Michael wrote and produced for Diana Ross, was actually named for his pet snake.

■ "Billie Jean" was written about an obsessive fan who insisted that Michael had fathered her child. Eventually she was committed to a psychiatric hospital.

■ While at Motown, the Jacksons recorded 469 songs. Of these, only 174 have ever been released.

■ Michael starred in a short film called *Captain Eo*, playing an intergalactic traveler with a crew of puppets. The film plays at Disneyland and Disney World in theaters built especially for it.

■ Michael won a Grammy for his work on

E.T., a children's album telling the story of E.T., the extraterrestrial.

■ While the Jackson Five's *Christmas Album* was an annual hit for three years in a row, the Jacksons do not actually celebrate Christmas. As Jehovah's Witnesses, they do not celebrate holidays or birthdays.

■ Paul McCartney performed with Michael on the album *Thriller*, singing "The Girl Is Mine." Michael returned the favor by singing "Say, Say, Say" with Paul on his album *Pipes of Peace*.

■ Paul McCartney inadvertently gave

Michael the idea to purchase ATV Music, which owned the rights to many Beatles songs. McCartney had wanted to buy the company with Yoko Ono and felt outraged and betrayed when Michael outbid him.

■ The day after his performance for Motown's twenty-fifth anniversary, Michael received a congratulatory call from Fred Astaire. The legendary dancer had enjoyed Michael's dancing performance so much that he had taped it.

■ Besides appearing as an animated cartoon on the Saturday morning TV show

"The Jackson Five," Michael was a Claymation "Raisin" for the California Raisin campaign and the voice for a character on the prime-time cartoon show "The Simpsons."

■ None of the songs from the Jacksons' *Victory* album was performed on their Victory Tour.

■ "One Bad Apple," a hit for the Osmonds, was originally written for the Jackson Five. "Ben," a platinum single for Michael Jackson, was originally intended for Donny Osmond.

■ "Even at home, I'm lonely. I sit in my room sometimes and cry. It's so hard to make friends, and there are some things you can't talk to your parents or family about. I sometimes walk around the neighborhood at night...hoping to find someone to talk to. But I just end up coming home."

■ "One of my favorite pastimes is being with children. . . . They're one of the main reasons I do what I do. They know everything that people are trying to find out—

they know so many secrets—but it's hard for them to get it out. . . . They go through a brilliant genius stage. But then, when they become a certain age, they lose it."

■ "I think I have had the most amazing education anyone could ask for. We saw things most kids our age never saw."

■ "It's beautiful at the shows when people join together. It's our own little world. For that hour and a half we try to show that there's hope and goodness. It's only when you step outside the building that you see all the craziness."

■ "When I get onstage, I don't know what happens. Honest to God. It feels so good, it's like it's the safest place in the world for me."

"All the things I've read in my schoolbooks about England and the queen were okay, but my very eyes are the greatest book in the world. When we did the royal command performance, and then after it I actually looked in the queen's eyes, it was the greatest thing!"

■ "I want my whole career to be the greatest show on earth."

QUOTES FROM
MICHAEL

Diana Ross Presents the Jackson 5

Christmas Album

The Jackson 5's Greatest Hits

Goin' Places

Motown Special Anthology

Destiny

Triumph

Victory
The Wiz cast album
Off the Wall
Thriller
E.T.
Bad
Dangerous

The Wiz full-length feature film

Captain Eo short feature film

"Billie Jean" video

"Beat It" video

"Thriller" short film

The Making of Michael Jackson's Thriller

"The Girl Is Mine" and "Say, Say, Say"
 duets with Paul McCartney

"We Are the World" (USA for Africa)
"Bad" video
"Smooth Criminal" video
Moonwalker
"Black and White" video

The text of this book has been set in Bodoni Book and Copperplate Gothic, by Aaron Coleman of Linoprint Composition in New York, New York.

■

Book design, layout and jacket design by Judith A. Stagnitto.

GW00706173